A Pocket Guide to

Purgatory

Dedicated to the holy souls
in purgatory.
May God grant them rest and peace,
and may perpetual light shine upon them.

A Pocket Guide to

Purgatory

Patrick Madrid

Our Sunday Visitor Publishing Division
Our Sunday Visitor, Inc.
Huntington, Indiana 46750

Copyright © 2007 by Patrick Madrid
11 10 09 08 07   1 2 3 4 5 6 7 8 9

Our Sunday Visitor Publishing Division
Our Sunday Visitor, Inc.
200 Noll Plaza
Huntington, IN 46750

ISBN: 978-1-59276-294-1(Inventory No. T384)
LCCN: 2006940379

Cover design by Tyler Ottinger
Cover photo: Image 100
Interior design by Sherri L. Hoffman

PRINTED IN THE UNITED STATES OF AMERICA

Contents

I had never heard of a "papoose board" before the day I watched my three-year-old son, Timothy, being strapped onto one.

A neighbor kid had been swinging a toy around and accidentally smacked Tim in the face with it, opening a deep wound above his right eye that bled profusely. This wasn't something a bandage could fix. It was clear that Tim was going to need several stitches to close the gash, so my wife and I scrambled him into the car and bolted for the hospital.

The blood, the pain, and the look of deep worry on his parents' faces were enough to keep Tim whimpering all the way to the emergency room. But once we got there, and my wife handed him to the nurses, his whimpering spiked into a wail of fright and pain as they laid his twisting little body on the board and tightly laced its cloth flaps in place, immobilizing him.

Within moments, the doctor had arrived and began to work on repairing Tim's wounded face. "*Mommmmy!*" our little boy shrieked, red-faced and wide-eyed, as he writhed in pain within the confines of the papoose board. "Help me, Mommy! It hurts!"

My wife and I stood by in anguish, unable to help him, watching the doctor clean and stitch the wound. It hurt us terribly to see him so scared and in pain, but we knew we had to let our son undergo this painful and frightening procedure — that we were actually doing what was best for him. The doctor could cure him, but only at the price of the pain involved in stitching the wound. (The doctor did a good job. After the wound healed, there wasn't even a scar to show for it.)

That incident happened many years ago, but the lessons I learned about pain and love have stayed with me vividly since then. My wife and I wanted to stop Tim's pain because we loved him, but we also knew that if he underwent the painful process in the emergency room, he would be much better off for it. So, out of our love for him, we had to let him face the pain so that the best thing for him — healing — could take place. It was hard, but it was necessary.

This is true of purgatory as well. God is a Father who loves us far beyond our ability to imagine, and he wants what's best for each of us. In some cases, what's best involves the suffering that necessarily comes with the healing purification, or *purging*, from sin and its effects on the soul.

This little book will take you on a guided tour of the scriptural evidence for purgatory and will consider what the early Christians believed on the subject. But before we delve into the finer details of what this means, let's first step back and get a "big picture" look at what purgatory is (and isn't).

I.

Purgatory: What It Is (and Isn't)

What exactly is purgatory?

The Catholic Church teaches that purgatory is a temporary state of purification for those who die in the state of grace and friendship with God (cf. Rom. 11:22), but who still have the vestiges of temporal effects due to sin, inordinate attachment to creatures, and whose will is not fully united with God's will. This purification involves suffering (St. Paul uses the analogy of fire to emphasize this), as God's fiery love "burns" away all impurities that may remain. Once this is complete, the soul enters into God's presence, the beatific vision, in which the perfect bliss of beholding Him face-to-face lasts forever.

You can think of purgatory as a kind of divine emergency room for souls, the process through which God, the Divine Physician, removes all traces of venial sins unrepented before death and heals the self-inflicted wounds of serious sin that we accumulate in this life. In purgatory, our wounds are healed, the scars are erased, and our souls are scrubbed clean by God's fiery love, washed white as snow by the shed Blood of the Lamb, made ready to enter into the eternal wedding feast we call heaven.[1]

Is purgatory biblical?

Yes. Evidence for it is wide and deep in Scripture, as we shall soon see. The belief is also well-attested to over the course of the 2,000-year history of the Catholic Church, in particular in the writings of the early Christians, including many of the early Church Fathers.

Some non-Catholic Christians — including most Protestants — regard purgatory as an offensive doctrine. They see it as conflicting with the truth that Christ died "once for all" for our sins.[2] Arguments against purgatory range from the "It's not taught in the Bible" variety to the "It denigrates the finished redemptive work of Christ on the Cross"[3] variety.

For example, a non-Catholic might ask, "If Jesus Christ died 'once for all' (as the Bible says he did in passages such as Heb. 7:27, 10:14, and 1 Pet. 3:18), why then do Catholics think someone needs to suffer in purgatory for his sins? Wasn't His death sufficient to save us from our sins?"

This is a fair question, and to answer it properly, we must be careful to examine several key issues that are part of the "bigger picture" of purgatory. Part of this bigger picture is coming to understand what purgatory is *not*.

Misconceptions about what the Catholic Church really teaches about purgatory are often the basis for Protestant objections. Clear those misconceptions up, and you're well on your way to helping them see the truth of this important biblical doctrine.

What purgatory is *not*

First, purgatory is not a place where people go to get a "second chance" from God, as

Hebrews. 9:27 makes clear: *It is appointed for men to die once, and after that comes judgment.* In addition to being a good verse to bring up when someone poses the possibility of reincarnation, it's also a good clarification of the fact that purgatory doesn't involve some kind of "second chance."

The *Catechism of the Catholic Church* states:

> . . . death is the end of man's earthly pilgrimage, of the time of grace and mercy which God offers him so as to work out his earthly life in keeping with the divine plan and to decide his ultimate destiny. . . . Death puts an end to human life as the time open to either accepting or rejecting the divine grace manifested in Christ.[4] The New Testament speaks of judgment primarily in its aspect of the final encounter with Christ in his second coming, but also repeatedly affirms that each will be rewarded immediately after death in accordance with his works and faith.[5]

Second, purgatory is not a place where the soul works, earns, or in any other way *does* something to cleanse himself; all purification that takes place in purgatory is done *by God* to the soul. Those who go to purgatory are assured of their salvation; there is nothing for them to do — Christ does it all in His merciful act of preparing His beloved to enter into the wedding feast. The *Catechism* states:

> *All who die in God's grace and friendship,*[6] *but still imperfectly purified, are indeed assured of their eternal salvation; but after death they undergo purification, so as to achieve the holiness necessary to enter the joy of heaven.*[7]

— *CCC* 1030

Third, purgatory is not where people end up who are "too good" to go to hell and "not good enough" to go to heaven. This is a third common misunderstanding of this doctrine. There is no such thing as a "middle ground" when it comes to salvation. As Christ explained in His teaching about the sheep and the goats in Matt. 25:31-46, there are only two ultimate eternal destinations, heaven and hell. St. Paul emphasizes this when he says:

> *For he will render to every man according to his works: to those who by patience in well-doing seek for glory and honor and immortality, he will give eternal life; but for those who are factious and do not obey the truth, but obey wickedness, there will be wrath and fury.*[8]

Since there are only two ultimate destinies possible for all human beings, heaven or hell, the issue of purgatory must be understood as simply a part of the process for some souls destined for heaven. If you die unrepentant in the state of mortal sin, you will go to hell.[9] If you die in the state of grace and friendship with God, you will go to heaven. You may first need to be purified of any lingering sins or selfishness, however minor, that would block your complete union with the all-holy God, but that purification — purgatory — is simply a temporary prelude to your receiving your eternal reward.

Okay, so what *is* purgatory?

Purgatory is a finite process[10] of purification, carried out by God, through His fiery love, on the soul of one who has died in the state of grace and is destined for heaven. It has no connection with the infinite penalty (hell) merited by our sin. Only Jesus Christ, through His saving death on the cross, is capable of expiating and remitting the eternal penalties due to our sins. Purgatory deals with the *side effects* of sins that may remain.

In 1 Cor. 3, St. Paul described this final purification[11] performed by God on the soul of a departed Christian, a process that that involves suffering:

> *According to the commission of God given to me, like a skilled master builder I laid a foundation, and another man is building upon it. Let each man take care how he builds upon it. For no other foundation can any one lay than that which is laid,*

which is Jesus Christ. Now if any one builds on the foundation with gold, silver, precious stones, wood, hay, stubble — each man's work will become manifest; for the Day will disclose it, because it will be revealed with fire, and the fire will test what sort of work each one has done. If the work which any man has built on the foundation survives, he will receive a reward. If any man's work is burned up, he will suffer loss, though he himself will be saved, but only as through fire.

— 1 COR. 3:10-15

Purgatory purges away all the dross that clings to the soul, things that St. Paul describes metaphorically as flammable materials such as "wood, hay, and straw." Conversely, that man's good works — which St. Paul compares with "gold, silver, and precious stones" — are refined and retained.

Is purgatory a Catholic doctrine or just a pious tradition?

Purgatory is a formally declared doctrine of the Catholic Church. It has been part of the deposit of faith "once for all handed down to the holy ones" (Jude 3) since the time of the Apostles. Purgatory is part of the Sacred Tradition of the Church; it is clearly taught in Scripture; and it was clearly taught by the early Church councils and the early Church Fathers.[12]

2.

Is purgatory found in the Bible?

Yes. Although the word "purgatory" isn't found in the Bible, many non-Catholics are surprised when they discover that the *teaching* regarding purgatory is clearly there, both implicitly and explicitly. But before we consider the New Testament evidence, let's first look at the main Old Testament passage that points to the reality of suffering of the departed being mitigated (i.e., lessened) through the prayers and sacrifice made on their behalf by those here on earth.

The twelfth chapter of 2 Maccabees contains an episode in which sacrifices are made in the temple on behalf of dead soldiers who were punished for the sin of superstition. The chapter concludes with the words:

> *In doing this he [Judas Maccabeus] acted very well and honorably, taking account of the resurrection. For if he were not*

expecting that those who had fallen would rise again, it would have been superfluous and foolish to pray for the dead. But if he was looking to the splendid reward that is laid up for those who fall asleep in godliness, it was a holy and pious thought. Therefore he made atonement for the dead, that they might be delivered from their sin.

— 2 MACC. 12:43-45

Unfortunately, since some non-Catholics (including most Protestants) erroneously exclude 2 Maccabees from the Old Testament canon, quoting that passage won't cut much ice with them. You may as well be quoting from the Yellow Pages. So we turn now to the New Testament.

Luke 16:19-31

In Luke 16, Christ mentions a third state after death — not heaven, not hell — where he discussed the temporary fates of Lazarus and the Rich Man:

"There was a rich man, who was clothed in purple and fine linen and who feasted sumptuously every day. And at his gate lay a poor man named Lazarus, full of sores, who desired to be fed with what fell from the rich man's table; moreover the dogs came and licked his sores.

"The poor man died and was carried by the angels to Abraham's bosom. The rich man also died and was buried; and in Hades, being in torment, he lifted up his eyes, and saw Abraham far off and Lazarus in his bosom. And he called out, 'Father Abraham, have mercy upon me, and send Lazarus to dip the end of his finger in water and cool my tongue; for I am in anguish in this flame.'

"But Abraham said, 'Son, remember that you in your lifetime received your good things, and Lazarus in like manner evil things; but now he is comforted here, and you are in anguish. And besides all this, between us and you a great chasm has been fixed, in order that those who would *pass from here to you may not be able, and none may cross from there to us.'*

"And he said, 'Then I beg you, father, to send him to my father's house, for I have five brothers, so that he may warn them, lest they also come into this place of torment.' But Abraham said, 'They have Moses and the prophets; let them hear them.' And he said, 'No, father Abraham; but if some one goes to them from the dead, they will repent.' He said to him, 'If they do not hear Moses and the prophets, neither will they be convinced if some one should rise from the dead.'"

— LUKE16:19-31

Where were Lazarus and the Rich Man?

It is clear that Abraham and Lazarus were not in hell, but neither were they in heaven. Remember, the Lord Jesus Christ had not yet died on the cross, so the gates of heaven were still closed to all those righteous men and women who died before Christ's saving work (cf. 1 Pet. 3:18-20, 4:6). These two men were in a special place of waiting (what theologians sometimes call the "Limbo of the Fathers"). This was the place (or state) in which the souls of the just anxiously awaited Christ's redemptive sacrifice on the cross that would enable them to finally enter into heaven.[13]

Notice a striking element of this passage: Christ tells us that the Rich Man was interceding on behalf of his brothers who were still alive. Christ himself gives us the evidence of a deceased person interceding on behalf of the living.

Now, this might indicate that the Rich Man, although in a place of "fiery torment," may not have been in the hell of the damned (cf. Matt. 25). After all, the damned are incapable of showing true charity, and the Rich Man was clearly doing so. He may actually have been being purified, since he was praying for his brothers.

Matthew 12:32

In this passage, Christ mentions a sin that cannot be forgiven even "in the world to come," implying that there are some sins that will be forgiven after death (St. Augustine interpreted this passage this way, with regard to purgatory, in *City of God* 21:24:2). Similarly, in the teaching about the Wicked Servant, Christ concludes with the fact that, even after his debt was canceled by the king, this servant was thrown into prison for maltreating his fellow servant and told:

> *"'You wicked servant! I forgave you all that debt because you besought me; and should not you have had mercy on your fellow servant, as I had mercy on you?' And in anger his lord delivered him to the jailers, till he should pay all his debt."*
>
> — MATT. 18:32-34

Then Christ adds this warning to us:

> *"So also my heavenly Father will do to every one of you, if you do not forgive your brother from your heart."*
>
> — MATT. 18:35

Echoing this theme, St. Peter speaks about the souls who are "in prison," awaiting their entrance into heaven (cf. 1 Pet. 3:18-19, 4:6). The process of cleansing we Catholics call "purgatory" (from the Latin word *purgare,* which means "to clean," or "to purify") involves pain, but it is necessary for God to make us pure, clean, and whole, ready to meet him face-to-face.

But doesn't the Bible say "to be absent from the body is to be present with the Lord?"

No. Sometimes Protestants will erroneously invoke two passages, 2 Cor. 5:6-8 and Phil. 1:21-23, to disprove Catholic teaching.[14] Their argument goes like this: "The Bible says that 'to be absent from the body means to be present with the Lord.' So there is no biblical basis for thinking a Christian can go to any other location (such as purgatory)."

But this argument is based on a simple mis-quoting of the texts. Look what they actually say:

> *So we are always of good courage; we know that **while we are at home in the body we are away from the Lord**, for we walk*

*by faith, not by sight. We are of good courage, and **we would rather be away from the body and at home with the Lord**. So whether we are at home or away, we make it our aim to please Him. For we must all appear before the judgment seat of Christ, so that each one may receive good or evil, according to what he has done in the body.*

—2 COR. 5:6-8 (emphasis added)

For to me to live is Christ, and to die is gain. If it is to be life in the flesh, that means fruitful labor for me. Yet which I shall choose I cannot tell. I am hard pressed between the two. My desire is to depart and be with Christ, for that is far better.

— PHIL. 1:21-23

As you can see, these texts say nothing whatsoever that would exclude purgatory, in that they're not saying that after death, a person goes immediately to heaven. Purgatory is quite compatible with these passages (when they are quoted correctly, of course).

But if Christ died for our sins, why must anyone go to purgatory?

Remember what the *Catechism* says:

> *All who die in God's grace and friendship, but still imperfectly purified, are indeed assured of their eternal salvation; but after death they undergo purification, so as to achieve the holiness necessary to enter the joy of heaven.*
>
> — *CCC* 1030

This refers to the fact about heaven that *Nothing unclean shall enter it, nor any one who practices abomination or falsehood, but only those who are written in the Lamb's book of life* (Rev. 21:27).

Why can nothing unclean enter heaven? The prophet Habakkuk says it's because God is all holy, and He will not allow anything in heaven with Him to be less than holy and spotless: *Too pure are your eyes to look upon evil [O*

LORD], and the sight of misery you cannot endure (Hab. 1:13). What eliminates that impurity is what the Church calls purgatory — entirely different from the punishment of the damned.

Ironically, for holding a doctrine so inextricably associated with Catholicism, the Catholic Church itself has not said all that much, "officially," about purgatory. The Council of Trent (1535-1548) was the setting for the Church's formal definition of the doctrine of purgatory. Here's what the Council said:

> *Whereas the Catholic Church, instructed by the Holy Spirit, has, from the sacred writings and the ancient tradition of the Fathers, taught, in sacred councils, and very recently in this ecumenical Synod, that there is a Purgatory, and that the souls there detained are helped by the suffrages of the faithful, but principally by the acceptable sacrifice of the altar; the holy Synod enjoins on bishops that they diligently endeavor that the sound doctrine concerning Purgatory, transmitted by the holy Fathers and sacred councils, be believed,*

*maintained, taught, and every where pro-
claimed by the faithful of Christ.*

— SESSION 25, NOVEMBER 4, 1563

Two kinds of punishment?

Some people get mixed up at this point. They
wonder why there should be a purgatory at all,
given that Christ's work on the Cross completed His mission of redemption. After all, the
Lord Himself said, "It is finished"(*tetélestai*),
just before he died on the Cross (John 19:30).

But there are two issues at work here. The
eternal penalty due to sin is hell, but that is distinct from the other inevitable penalty that
arises from sin: namely, the aftereffects that
play out across space and time.

For example, let's say a married woman
commits the sin of adultery. The eternal
penalty incurred by her mortal (i.e., "deadly")
sin is the complete eradication of sanctifying
grace from her soul. She renders herself spiritually dead, as dead as if she had put a gun to her
head and pulled the trigger (cf. *CCC* 1849-

1864). The eternal penalty due to her sin (had she remained unrepentant and died in that state) would be the eternal death we call hell. But that penalty has been removed, washed away by the shed blood of Christ on the cross:

> *But he was wounded for our transgressions, he was bruised for our iniquities; upon him was the chastisement that made us whole, and with his stripes we are healed.*
>
> — Is. 53:5

> *But God shows his love for us in that while we were yet sinners Christ died for us. Since, therefore, we are now justified by his blood, much more shall we be saved by him from the wrath of God.*
>
> — Rom. 5:8-9

Therefore, the adulterous woman has the promise of forgiveness from Christ if she repents of her sin, and the Lord will reestablish the life of sanctifying grace in her soul when she receives the sacrament of confession (penance). She is forgiven and restored in a right relationship with God.

But her saga isn't over. Even though she is forgiven and back in the state of grace, the temporal effects of her sin remain. They were not eliminated by Christ's death on the cross.

There are many possible side effects of this kind of sin, and any of them could happen:

- Perhaps she became pregnant.
- Perhaps she contracted a sexually-transmitted disease.
- Perhaps her marriage was shattered as a result of her actions.

You see, the temporal *consequences* of her sin are not expunged, even though she has repented.

God wants the souls of His beloved sons and daughters to be perfect and clean, free of blemish or stain. When we sin, this "wounds" the soul. The wound may be healed through the sacraments, but a temporal "scar" remains and must also be expiated and removed.

The *Catechism* then quotes the teaching of Pope St. Gregory the Great on purgatory:

> *As for certain lesser faults, we must believe that, before the Final Judgment there is a purifying fire. He who is truth says that whoever utters blasphemy against the Holy Spirit will be pardoned neither in this age nor in the age to come. From this sentence we understand that certain offenses can be forgiven in this age, but certain others in the age to come.*

> — ST. GREGORY THE GREAT,
> *DIALOGUE* 4:39

What's the difference between eternal and temporal effects of sin?

To understand more clearly the need for purification from the temporal punishments due to sin, let's rewind back to the beginning of human history, back to the Garden of Eden. When Adam and Eve committed the "Original Sin" in the Garden (cf. Gen. 3:1-7), they disrupted their intimate friendship with the Lord.

When they fell from grace, they not only lost many supernatural gifts of grace and union with God; they also lost many natural gifts, such as freedom from their passions, control over their will, and a preternaturally enhanced human knowledge. Their gift of immortality was taken away (cf. *CCC* 397-409).

And with that loss came a series of other "temporal punishments," consequences of their sin that continue, embedded in the human condition, down to our own day. Earlier, before the Fall, God had warned Adam and Eve about the result of sin:

> *"You may freely eat of every tree of the garden; but of the tree of the knowledge of good and evil you shall not eat, for in the day that you eat of it you shall die."*
>
> — GEN. 2:17

This truth was echoed by St. Paul when he said, "The wages of sin is death" (Rom. 6:23).

So death came for our first parents, in more ways than one. Spiritually, it can be said that they "died" that very day, because their life of grace and intimate union with God had vanished:

> ... the man and his wife hid themselves from the presence of the LORD God among the trees of the garden.
>
> But the LORD God called to the man, and said to him, "Where are you?" And he said, "I heard the sound of thee in the garden, and I was afraid, because I was naked; and I hid myself."

> — GEN. 3:8-10

We also see that, following on the heels of their spiritual death, a series of natural consequences also spelled disaster for humanity and all creation. Speaking first to the Serpent, God cursed him for his wickedness in tempting Adam and Eve.

Why did God pronounce these curses?

The LORD God said to the serpent,
"Because you have done this, cursed are
you above all cattle, and above all wild ani-
mals; upon your belly you shall go, and dust
you shall eat all the days of your life.

"I will put enmity between you and the
woman, and between your seed and her
seed; he shall bruise your head, and you
shall bruise his heel."

— GEN. 3:14-15

To the woman he said, "I will greatly mul-
tiply your pain in childbearing; in pain
you shall bring forth children, yet your
desire shall be for your husband, and he
shall rule over you."

And to Adam he said, "Because you
have listened to the voice of your wife, and
have eaten of the tree of which I com-
manded you, 'You shall not eat of it,'
cursed is the ground because of you; in toil
you shall eat of it all the days of your life;
thorns and thistles it shall bring forth to

you; and you shall eat the plants of the
field. In the sweat of your face you shall
eat bread till you return to the ground, for
out of it you were taken; you are dust, and
to dust you shall return."

— GEN. 3:16-19

Didn't Christ's saving death take away all punishments?

No. As God, Christ alone is the one who could pay the price for the eternal punishment due to our sins, but His death on the cross did not eliminate the temporal effects due to sin. Remember, Adam and Eve were forgiven of the eternal penalties of that sin, as is all the rest of humanity that repents and asks forgiveness. But the temporal effects due to their sin — sickness, suffering, labor, and death — remain (cf. *CCC* 1008, 1472, 1505).

This principle of a separate temporal punishment due to sin is seen throughout the Bible. A striking example is the tragic aftermath of King David's double-barreled sins of adultery and murder.

Nathan said to David, "You are the man. Thus says the Lord, the God of Israel, 'I anointed you king over Israel, and I delivered you out of the hand of Saul; and I gave you your master's house, and your master's wives into your bosom, and gave you the house of Israel and of Judah; and if this were too little, I would add to you as much more. Why have you despised the word of the Lord, to do what is evil in his sight?'" [. . .] David said to Nathan, "I have sinned against the Lord."

And Nathan said to David, "The Lord also has put away your sin; you shall not die. Nevertheless, because by this deed you have utterly scorned the Lord, the child that is born to you shall die."
— 2 SAM. 12:7-14 (cf. Num. 12:1-15, 22:12, 27:12-14)

Toil, pain, difficulty, sickness, death — these were all part of the declining arc of existence that Adam and Eve set themselves on when they disobeyed God. Distinct from the "eternal penalty" of hell, these penalties lie squarely in the category of what we Catholics call the "temporal effects" due to sin. The three direst consequences of Adam and Eve's Original Sin[15] are sickness, death, and concupiscence — a catastrophe in which you and I must share, since we are descended from Adam and Eve.[16]

The temporal effects due to sin extend, sadly, far beyond just physical illness and death.[17] They include the spiritual impurities and weaknesses that cling to the soul. So, in addition to being purged of these impurities, we may also have to make restitution as well.

Why would I have to make restitution?
Consider this analogy.

Let's imagine you had figured out a clever way to steal a very expensive, state-of-the-art "big screen" television from your local electronics emporium without getting caught. You steal the TV, get it home, and immediately begin feeling remorse over your crime. This step equates with the sinner whose conscience torments him, prodding him to repent.

Then, you feel so badly about what you've done, you go to the store, find the manager and confess that you stole the TV (this step equates with the sinner making a good act of contrition).

So . . . what if I'm forgiven? What then?

The store manager thinks for a moment and says, "I'll tell you what. By law, you are guilty of a felony. Regardless of the fact that you are here confessing to me, I could call the police and have you arrested. You would be tried in court and sentenced to a long, unpleasant prison term as punishment for your theft. You would forever have a felony on your record. You'd be barred from getting certain kinds of work, and your life would be ruined as a result of this theft" (this equates with God's just punishment that the sinner deserves).

Then, the manager smiles. "But, since you've confessed this crime, I'm not going to call the police. I'm not going to have you arrested and tried. There will be no jail for you. I will treat this as if it had never happened."

You are ready to faint with relief. Certainly, you don't deserve this forgiveness, but you're ecstatic. You're going to be let go without paying the penalty. But then, as you shake the store manager's hand gratefully and turn to leave the store, he taps you on the shoulder and adds, "Now, I'll expect you to bring the TV back to me today."

In other words, there's a pre-condition for this turn of events. You have to make *restitution* — replacement of the stolen item. Clearly, even though you've avoided the legal penalty your crime deserved, you still are obligated to return the TV to the store. And if you've damaged or sold it in the meantime, you're still obligated, as a matter of justice, to pay the sum equal to the value of the TV. If you don't, you are in effect nullifying the store manager's kindness.

Purgatory, then, is where some who die in the state of grace will make restitution for the temporal effects due to their forgiven sins.

3.

Purgatory and the Early Church

Did the early Christians believe in purgatory?

Yes, indeed, they did. In addition to the weight of biblical evidence for purgatory, it's important to realize that this doctrine was universally believed and taught in the early Church. This means that purgatory — far from being a "Catholic invention," as most Protestants assume — was believed from the very beginning by the early followers of Christ.

The most explicit extra-biblical evidence for the belief in the doctrine of purgatory in the ancient Church is found in its liturgies. Without exception, in the East and the West, the various eucharistic liturgies contained at least one *memento mori*, "remembrance of the dead."

Now, if the dead are either in heaven or hell, there's no point in praying for them. In heaven, they would have no need of prayer; in hell, prayer could do them no good. But the Church knew then, as she does now, that there is a "middle state" where those who die in the state of grace and are assured of their salvation can benefit from our prayers, the "middle state" of purgatory.

Catholic historian Edward J. Hanna points out a significant piece of historical evidence for the antiquity of the Christian belief in purgatory:

> *The teaching of the Fathers, and the formularies used in the Liturgy of the Church, found expression in the early Christian monuments, particularly those contained in the catacombs. On the tombs of the faithful were inscribed words of hope, words of petition for peace and for rest; and as the anniversaries came round the faithful gathered at the graves of the departed to make intercession for those*

*who had gone before. At the bottom this is
nothing else than the faith expressed by the
Council of Trent (Session 25, "On Purgatory"), and to this faith the inscriptions in
the catacombs are surely witnesses.*
— The Catholic Encyclopedia;
New York: Robert Appleton Co.,
1911, vol. 12, p. 577

The Fathers of the Church were adamant
about the existence of purgatory. Around the
year 392, St. John Chrysostom wrote about the
need for Christians to assist the souls of the
faithful departed through prayers:

*Let us help and commemorate them. If
Job's sons were purified by their father's sacrifice,*[18] *why would we doubt that our
offerings for the dead bring them some
consolation? Let us not hesitate to help
those who have died and to offer our
prayers for them.*[19]

St. Augustine also wrote frequently about
purgatory and the need for offering prayers for
the dead. Besides showing his own and the

early Church's recognition that 2 Maccabees is part of the Old Testament canon of inspired Scripture, he summarizes the early Church's teaching on purgatory and prayers for the dead in Christ:

> *We read in the book of Maccabees that the sacrifice was offered for the dead.[20] But even if it were found nowhere in the Old Testament writings, the authority of the universal Church which is clear on this point is of no small weight, where in the prayers of the priest poured forth to the Lord God at His altar the commendation of the dead has its place.[21]*
>
> — *ON THE CARE THAT SHOULD BE TAKEN FOR THE DEAD* 1:3; CF. 15:18

Some other Church Fathers' writings on purgatory:

- St. Ambrose, *Sermon Twenty on Psalms,* 117;

- St. Jerome, *Commentary on Amos,* 100:4;

- St. Augustine, *Commentary on Psalms* *37;*
- St. Cyril of Jerusalem, *Catechetical Lectures* 5:9;
- Pope St. Gregory the Great, *Dialogue 4,* 39;
- Origen, *Homily Six On Exodus;*
- St. Gregory of Nyssa, *Sermon on the Dead* (A.D. 382);
- St. John Chrysostom, *Homilies on the Epistle to the Philippians* 3:4-10 (A.D. 398);
- Serapion, *Prayer of the Eucharistic Sacrifice* 13:1-27 (A.D. 350).

The reason Christians have always prayed for the dead is because they have known, having learned it from the Apostles themselves, that many — perhaps most — who die in a state of friendship with God still must undergo a purification that involves suffering. Prayers on behalf of our deceased brothers and sisters in the Lord can help alleviate and even shorten that suffering.

4.

Purgatory and You

Feel the burn

No discussion of purgatory would be complete without mention of the ubiquitous image of fire. Despite persistent misconceptions to the contrary, this fire imagery is not a "medieval invention" of a "sadistic" Catholic Church, bent on frightening poor peasants into repentance. On the contrary, throughout Scripture, fire is frequently used as an image to explain God's wrath and punishment (as in the fires of hell, cf. Mt. 18:8-9, 25:41). But it also appears as a manifestation of His power, love, and presence — as in the burning bush with Moses (Ex. 3:2), the pillar of fire guiding the Israelites in the desert (Ex. 13:21), and tongues of flame that appeared over the heads of Mary and the Apostles on the Day of Pentecost (Acts 2:3).

Writing at the middle of the fourth century, St. Ambrose of Milan remarked about the Old

Testament's use of the "fire" image as the means of purifying one from evil speech:

> Now must I needs confess the Prophet Isaiah's confession, which he makes before declaring the word of the Lord: "Woe is me, my heart is smitten, for I, a man of unclean lips, and living in the midst of a people of unclean lips, have seen the Lord of Hosts." Now if Isaiah said "Woe is me," who looked upon the Lord of Hosts, what shall I say of myself, who, being "a man of unclean lips," am constrained to treat of the divine generation (i.e. explain the Trinitarian relationship of God the Son and God the Holy Spirit to God the Father)? How shall I break forth into speech of things whereof I am afraid, when David prays that a watch may be set over his mouth in the matter of things whereof he has knowledge? O that to me also one of the Seraphim would bring the burning coal from the celestial altar, taking it in the tongs of the two testaments

and with the fire thereof purge my unclean lips!

— *ON THE MYSTERIES*, 132

Perhaps the most pointed example of this fire imagery in Scripture is the statement, *Our God is a consuming fire!* (Heb. 12:29; cf. 2 Thess. 1:17). God's love for us consumes and burns away those things that keep us from complete union with him: inordinate self-love, attachment to things or other people, etc. In this life, His fiery love helps us rid ourselves of these base attachments through our acceptance and offering up of the sufferings that come our way.

How can suffering be good for me?

The Bible explains this paradox — that God, at times, sends suffering our way to help us:

And have you forgotten the exhortation which addresses you as sons? —

"My son, do not regard lightly the discipline of the Lord, nor lose courage when you are punished by him. For the Lord disci-

plines him whom he loves, and chastises every son whom he receives."

It is for discipline that you have to endure. God is treating you as sons; for what son is there whom his father does not discipline? If you are left without discipline, in which all have participated, then you are illegitimate children and not sons. Besides this, we have had earthly fathers to discipline us and we respected them. Shall we not much more be subject to the Father of spirits and live? For they disciplined us for a short time at their pleasure, but he disciplines us for our good, that we may share his holiness.

For the moment all discipline seems painful rather than pleasant; later it yields the peaceful fruit of righteousness to those who have been trained by it. Therefore list your drooping hands and strengthen your weak knees.

— HEB. 12:5-12

Once we enter into that final stage of judgment and our eternal reward, we come face-to-face with the burning love of the Triune God. Each of us will have to one day give an account of our lives to Christ, our Judge. Scripture says: *The Lord Jesus is revealed from heaven with his mighty angels in flaming fire* (2 Thess.1:7).

What did St. Paul teach about purgatory?
As we have seen, St. Paul taught the doctrine of purgatory using the image of fire (1 Cor. 3:10-15, quoted on pp. 17-18). Let's break this teaching on purgatory down to its basic components:

First, this passage deals with events taking place after death, on "the day" of a man's judgment (cf. Heb. 9:27, "It is appointed for men to die once, and after that comes judgment").

Second, the metaphor of fire St. Paul uses here describes the way in which God tests a man's life and "burns away" the dross. Just as fire consumes, destroys, and eliminates flammable objects (wood, hay, straw) — and, conversely, refines and purifies precious metals (gold and silver) — so goes the soul's progress at this point. Remember that the Latin word *purgare*, from which we derive the English word "purgatory," literally means "to cleanse" or "to purify." This is exactly what happens in purgatory. The soul of the man St. Paul describes as one who "built on the foundation of Christ" (i.e., in the state of grace and friendship with God)[22] is being purified by God's fiery love.

Third, this process involves loss and *suffering*. This element — the suffering — is perhaps the most controversial aspect of the historic Christian doctrine of purgatory, because those who reject it do so out of a sense that Christ's suffering and death on the Cross are being somehow impugned or minimized. But this is not at all the case.

Fourth, this process is temporary, culminating in the release of the soul from this state, his entrance into heaven, and his partaking in the beatific vision: seeing God face-to-face.[23]

As far as the fire goes, we can be content with saying that Scripture and the early Church Fathers used the image of fire to convey the painful, if temporary, reality of what happens in purgatory. Is it "real" fire? Probably not, at least not as we understand fire in a physical sense. Will this process hurt? Yes, as St. Paul says in 1 Cor. 3:15.

But perhaps the most important lesson we can learn from these facts is that we can avoid purgatory altogether, or at least an extended stay there, by offering to the Lord our daily trials and pains. These sufferings are purgatorial in themselves, if they are offered to God with a loving and contrite heart. In this way, our suffering is purified and elevated. It becomes a participation in the redemptive sufferings of Jesus Christ (cf. Col. 1:24).

Does everyone have to go to purgatory?

Whether or not you need to pass through the purifying flames of purgatory depends on decisions you make now. If you leave this world with clinging weeds of inordinate self-love, attachment to creatures, and venially sinful bad habits, you will need those weeds cut away and burned off before you can enter heaven. If your soul bears the scars of the self-inflicted wounds of mortal sin, you'll need those scars removed by the Divine Physician.

It hurts, yes. But it hurts so good, because we know that this process is bringing us closer to Christ, closer to that moment when we can enter the wedding feast of the Lamb, spotless and pure (Rev. 19:7-9).

Just as my wife and I let our son Timothy endure the pain of having his wounded eye cleaned and stitched up by the doctor in the emergency room so he could heal properly, so too, God permits us to suffer the consequences of sin. Through purgatory, He heals the wounds our sins have caused. Through the pain and suffering "as if passing through fire" that St. Paul speaks about, the Lord makes us whole again, ready to be with Him forever, face-to-face.

5.

Purgatory and Others

Can our prayers and penances help those in purgatory?

Yes. The plain reading of passages such as 2 Cor. 4:10, Phil. 3:10, and Col. 1:24 reveal that our sufferings (e.g., penances) can be beneficial to others:[24]

> *[We are] always carrying in the body the death of Jesus, so that the life of Jesus may also be manifested in our bodies.*
>
> — 2 COR. 4:10

> *[T]hat I may know him and the power of his resurrection, and may share his sufferings, becoming like him in his death.*
>
> — PHIL. 3:10

> *Now I rejoice in my sufferings for your sake, and in my flesh I complete what is*

lacking in Christ's afflictions for the sake of his body, that is, the church.
— COL. 1:24

Notice that St. Paul declares the value of *"my* sufferings for *your* sake."The penances of those who are united to Christ and "share in His sufferings, becoming like Him," have real value and true merit[25] in the eyes of God and can be applied to the benefit of others.

Some Protestants, though, blur the clear meaning of these passages in confusion regarding the two distinct categories of suffering: first, Christ's own unique, ineffable sacrifice, complete with His merits and expiation won for us through His suffering and death; second, our own human sufferings which, when united with Christ's, can have real merit and can benefit others.

The unfortunate error many Protestants fall into is to assume that *only* the infinitely meritorious sacrifice of Christ is being discussed in the passages above. Christ's sacrifice on the cross is utterly distinct from any sacrifices that we might make to the Lord (c.f., Rom. 12:1; Phil. 2:17, 4:18; Heb. 13:15). Christians can, however, *participate* in the sufferings of the Lord, always in a subordinate way, for the benefit of other members of the Body of Christ (c.f. 1 Cor. 12:12-26), including those in purgatory.

As St. Paul reminds us:

> *For as we share abundantly in Christ's sufferings, so through Christ we share abundantly in comfort too. If we are afflicted, it is for your comfort and salvation; and if we are comforted, it is for your comfort, which you experience when you patiently endure the same sufferings that we suffer. Our hope for you is unshaken; for we know that as you share in our sufferings, you will also share in our comfort.*

— 2 COR. 1:5-7

Notes

¹ Cf. Rev. 21:2, 9.

² Cf. Heb. 7:27, 9:27-28; 10:10.

³ Cf. John 19:30.

⁴ Cf. 2 Tim. 1:9-10.

⁵ *CCC* 1013; cf. 1021.

⁶ Cf. Rom. 2:6-7, 11:22.

⁷ The evidence is overwhelming that demonstrates that the early Church believed and taught the doctrine of purgatory and the concomitant doctrine that the prayers of the living can assist the faithful departed. E.g., Tertullian, *On The Soul* 58:1-2 (A.D. 208); St. Basil the Great, *Homilies on the Psalms* 7:2, 6 (A.D. 375); St. Gregory of Nyssa, *Sermon on the Dead* (A.D. 382); St. John Chrysostom, *Homilies on the Epistle to the Philippians* 3:4-10 (A.D. 398); Serapion, *Prayer of the Eucharistic Sacrifice* 13:1-27 (A.D. 350).

⁸ Rom. 2:6-8.

⁹ Cf. *CCC* 1861.

¹⁰ Historically, the doctors, Fathers, and theologians of the Church have also commonly referred to purgatory as a "place" and a "state," though the question of what is meant by "place," with regard to location and extension, is not part of this study.

¹¹ Cf. *CCC* 1031.

¹² Cf. Council of Lyons (1245); Council of Florence (1439); Council of Trent (1563), session 25.

¹³ Cf. Heb. 11:13-16, 32-40; 1 Pet. 3:18-22, 4:6.

¹⁴ Examples of this deliberate and apparently deceitful verse-quoting sleight-of-hand are found in Loraine Boettner, *Roman Catholicism*, 226; James G. McCarthy, *The Gospel According to Rome*, 120.

¹⁵ Cf. Gen. 2:15-17, 3:1-19.

¹⁶ Cf. *CCC* 404.

[17] In 1 Cor. 11:27-32, St. Paul warns that certain sins can have lethal side effects.

[18] Cf. Job 1:5.

[19] *Homilies on First Corinthians* 41:5; cf. Tertullian, *The Crown* 3:4 (A.D. 211); *On Monogamy* 10:1-4 (A.D. 213).

[20] 2 Macc. 12:39-43.

[21] *The Care That Should Be Taken for the Dead* 1:3; cf. 15:18.

[22] St. Paul refers to the necessity of remaining in the "state of grace" when he speaks about our remaining in the "kindness of God": "See, then, the kindness and severity of God: severity toward those who fell, but God's kindness to you, provided you remain in his kindness; otherwise you too will be cut off" (Rom.11:22). This admonition, which was addressed specifically to Christians, contains two truths: *if* you remain in God's grace you will be saved; *if* you choose to depart from his grace and die unrepentant in that state (i.e., grave sin, cf. Heb. 10:24-29; 2 Pet. 2:20-21; 1 Jn. 5:16-17), you will not be saved.

[23] The Greek word used here is the future tense verb *sothésetai,* showing that entrance into "final salvation" (i.e., what Christians have historically called "the beatific vision") is an event that takes place after this temporary process of suffering is completed.

[24] For a fuller explanation of how our prayers can assist those detained in purgatory, see Pope Paul VI's apostolic constitution *Indulgentiarum Doctrina* (www.vatican.va).

[25] Scripture is clear that good works, performed by Christians are meritorious in God's eyes (c.f., Matt. 5:12, 19:29, 25:31-46; Luke 6:38; Rom. 2:6; 1 Cor. 3:8; Heb. 10:35, 11:6). Early Church Fathers, such as Ignatius of Antioch, Justin Martyr, and Augustine were emphatic that merit can be acquired and applied by God to the benefit of others.

A lifelong Catholic, Patrick Madrid is an author of many books on Catholic themes and the editor of the apologetics online magazine **envoymagazine.com.** The host of four EWTN television programs and the Thursday edition of EWTN Radio's "Open Line" call-in broadcast, he conducts numerous apologetics seminars each year at parishes and universities across the United States and around the world.

Patrick and his wife, Nancy, have been blessed with eleven happy, healthy children.

For a complete listing of all Patrick's books, CDs, DVDs, and parish seminar topics, please visit: **www.patrickmadrid.com.**